BLESSINGS of
ETERNITY

poems
by

FRANK GABRIEL
DIFILIA

To
Curt
you have given
me so much
thank you
— C. DiFoli

Blessings of Eternity

the beauty that the poet sees
in scattered leaves and proud tall trees,
in love's sweet light and mysteries,
in people's lives, their deaths, their families,
their songs, their dance, their poetry,
in the history of all humankind,
in the rhythm and the rhyme of time,
in clouds adrift across open skies,
in nights aglow with stars and dreams,
in dogs and cats, the birds and bees,
in moonlight cast down on the seas,
in sunlight cast on you and me

the beauty that the poet hears
in seawaves as they disappear,
in people's laughter and their tears,
in streams, in wind, in rain, in storms,
in birdsong and the music of the spheres,
in young men's cries of victory,
in women's sighs of ecstasy,
in all our silent hopes and prayers

the sunrise and sunset,
the stars in dark night skies,
the sweet moonlight, our loves,
our lives, the miracle of you and me,
these are the blessings of eternity
blessings for all to hear and see

the trees please me
they sway so gently
and pray so proudly
free and stationary
intertwined with time

the past is my mother
the future my father
and I am their child
the present

my mother makes me what I am
my father what I can be
and I am their sea
mother makes me wet
father keeps me dry
and I am their sky
mother makes me light at night
father bright by day
and I am their clay
mother molds me caressingly
father with a chisel
and I am their pistol
mother unloads me with love
father fires me empty at false enemies

and so I ask
will you wonder first
or will you wonder last
before the time is past, or after

In the June month of 71
I set out sailing towards the sun
in a boat that could barely float

I knew the Isle of Death be
my destiny, my vessel would
wreak there ultimately, so
my soul had to seek the
realm of eternity

The third day out it began to rain,
fresh wet thoughts on my dried
out brain, elaborate patterns
formed on my mind's windowpane,
a poem came:

the soul is the sea of reality
don't swim with rationality
float with sensitivity,
float free, there is sunken
treasure for you to see

you won't find it by standing on the shore anymore

you must let yourself
be washed away

dark stays the night

and fashioned with fright

til by the light of love's insight
she is bejewelled bright

the stars are ours

light from above

to show us

the way to love

entranced in love began our dance
last night entranced we danced together
,

your soul and mine sublime in sacred meeting,

our bodies greeting with caresses of longing,
longing for wisdom, longing for love, longing
for life,

knowing to gain is to give not take,
knowing to love is to create, knowing to
create is to find the soul of reality,
knowing to be free is reality,
knowing each other as lovers only can,
knowing each other as woman and man

last night we danced on moonlit shores,
your soul and mine ...

she was a creature
who wanted to love

he really wanted to fly

darkness arose the deep night did close
her arms around us, we wept as we
walked, we talked and we sought to
reach the high mountains before us
too much thought had led us astray
now we fought to find our way
no questions to ask, only to
walk, and wonder

we knew that worlds revolve around worlds
we knew the moon makes tides in seas
we knew that men and women loved
and yet it seemed still that you
were only you and I only me

the tears that poured from the flow of your soul
was a flood of love you couldn't let go of
alone, for years you bore all your fears
of the world on your own

you wore them well, like a stunning
stone statue cast in hell, chiseled by
men's confusion and exclusion of thy beauty
you found refuse with the trees and
freedom for your seas

with the blazing heat of hurt were
you infused with your whole worth
and with the hotter heat of love
you shall melt to that worth's birth

you are a river not a rock
you are a giver, do not lock
the love of life within your soul,
even though you have been rolled
thru man's most miserable molds
with the fire of love shall you
now melt and of your beauty
make a boat so men again
may start to float far from
the miseries they wrote and
which you have so deeply felt

now must you give them thy help

shadowbird

blackbird of beauty

wild and wise like the wind
in the sky, she flies high
above a sea of humanity

with centuries of sensuousness
alive in her body
and eyes

Down with my self constructed death dam
it stems the flow of my spirit's waters

a man's demons must be drowned by the man

I am, therefore I am,
therefore I think,
therefore I feel,
I create,
I dream,
I love

...

and now I give to you a poem,
for then I left you all alone

her soft sweet breast caressed my hand
invoking me to understand the breath
of love within each breath she bravely
breathed upon my chest, a baited
breeze to be retrieved as poems
of love returning eternally

And so our love begins again
a love that ever could not end
and so our love begins anew
the love between we two

for then I left you all alone
and now you give to me this poem

So few men come with me
to sail the windy sea
So few men come with me
and fly to become free

Come sing with me in harmony
and like the waves upon the sea
our song will carry to the shore
of some men's souls and even more
into the ears of all who stroll
sometimes so near that shore

Like water is wound within the sea,
so bound together by soul are we

We are all leaves from the same tree
We are all streams flowing to the same sea

Come with me
Come with me

the world within each one of us

is filled with beauty, truth, and trust

and along its paths I wish to go

over the mountains high and

thru the valleys low, let the

winds within blow me to and fro

for across these seas I wish to sail

before these mysteries I'll stand

it is this world I want to know
it is this world I want to show

the lady of rainbow light

she floats thru a life of
a thousand dreams, and the
light of a thousand rainbows
streams forth from her soul

to bathe us clean and
make us whole ...

See
the universe
in space

dance
with
grace

love each
other

be
my
lover

a moonbeam is part of the sun's dreams
all we see is not what it first seems

a student once asked, where can one
truly find food for the soul,
his teacher replied, be still
and eat all the rice in your bowl

the night

tells her stories

in darkness
and in dreams

listen both to the
darkness
and
the dreams

a dream is a beam of beauty
that streams from the soul

can a dream only seem

never having ever been

never having ever
never having
never ...

I have laid with loneliness
I've felt the passion
of her kiss
I've seen desire in her eyes
I've touched
the fire
between her thighs

yes, I have laid with loneliness
and shared a deep caress ...

the moon came in my room last night
and lay upon the bed
she shook her
head and
crimson curls of light
spread across the pillows

she murmured something
soft and low
I heard
a moan within my soul
and we made love

we sailed so high
thru that night sky
in ecstasy
the moon and I

we lay on your couch
    that sunny afternoon
       trying to decide whether
         to make love or have a
            picnic at the lake

         we reach for a moment
         of infinite peace

         together

at dawn

I sit in meditation

sunlight
fills the room

sunny day in the park

children playing

I write haiku

love is like flowers
    or leaves on the trees
love is like moonlight,
    or sunlight, or dark night

      love is a game that
        everyone wins and nobody loses
      or everybody loses and
        nobody wins...

          love is a dream undone
          by the dawn, or a dream
          you dream on and on

I love you because the trees
grow tall outside my window
     and in the fall
      their leaves
drift to the ground

I love you because the light
from stars travels so fast
                              so far
                    each night to kiss our eyes

I love you because the sky is
such a lovely blue
some summer days and seems so high
                              and clear and wide

     I love you because the wind
      blows sometimes so gently
                    no one even knows ...

the love that you feel is real

the hate you create doth steal

the very life from your soul

til you are left alone and old
til you are left stiff and cold
til you are left rife with mold
til you are left dust of death

let your love grow
let your love flow

the old man stands and brushes
dirt from his weathered hands
he gazes upward to the sky
and memories of joys and
sorrows he once knew,
like clouds go slowly
drifting by in his
mind's eye

anew he is reminded of
the mystery of life
and death
and love

she came again one winter day
snow had fallen for several hours
and lay like a thick rug upon the ground

we sat by the fire and drank tea
the fire warmed and soothed us
we sat in silence as it burned down

she started to go and we kissed
like two leaves in autumn briefly
touching on their sweet and gentle
flight from the trees to the ground

the next day when I went outside
I could see no trace of her
departure in the freshly
fallen snow

I see her there on distant shores
her head held high above the sky
her body lithe, her feet tread
softly on the sand

I see her face, her lips, her eyes
and realize love never dies
it grows and blossoms
each moonrise

we stood kissing in the rain
when we first met, and when
it rained again we laughed
to find that we were kissing

now rain
always reminds me
of your eyes,
so clear so blue,

and I wish I was
kissing you

whisper to me
O Wind

whisper to me what you have to say

whisper to me O Wind

whisper to me then

be on your way and

whisper
to him

the wind
blows thru me

like a tree
beneath the sun

I stand
in awe
and wonder

Cosmic Consciousness

we are all of the same universe
said the whurple to the phig
just because my nose is missing
while yours is very big
that's no reason, that's no reason
for us to hate and more
that's no reason, that's no reason
for us to go to war

we are all of the same universe
said the brock to the cou
just because my skin is yellow
while yours is kinda blue
that's no reason, that's no reason
for us to hate and more
that's no reason, that's no reason
for us to go to war

we are all of the same universe
said one to the other
with God as our father and
Nature as our mother so
there's no reason, there's no reason
for us to hate and more
there's no reason, there's never a reason
for us to go to war

trees in their tall silence

taught me how to live

grow deep down into
  the ground and

    reach
          up high
                into
                    the sky

fire

with its
proud dance
of delight

taught me how
to love

so soft the glow
of the candlelake

so soft our love
so sweet our fate

so soft as stars
in nightsky wake

so soft …

my poem to the birds
is
a whistle without words

my poem to the trees
is
to climb them, if they please

my poem to the rocks
is
to sit atop them
with great honor

my poem to the stream
is
to listen,
still and silent

standing in
a cathedral of trees

silence
and sunlight
everywhere

then a warm
summer breeze
makes a choir
of some leaves

I feel a presence all around
I feel I walk on sacred ground

the earth
is my church

the philosophy of trees:
I stand, therefore I am

in the poetry of trees
love sonnets to the sun
are written on the breeze

in the religion of trees
the only prayer is
just to breathe

in a dream of mine
we kissed one time

and I could feel the
depth and breath of
our two hearts
rhyme

our souls can dance
thru this lifetime and
many more to come
as one

in moonlight by the sea, a
dark haired woman danced
a dance of loneliness
and love for me

her feet caressed the earth
her beauty blessed the sky
and her body expressed
the poetry of love

her radiance cast a spell on me
and I was captured in a moment
of eternal ecstasy

the moon cries "oh my"
the sea sighs "is that so"
the wind asks "but why"
the night replies "who knows"

then the sun comes dancing in
with a really bright grin and says
"hey cats, let's blow"

an eagle soars high

thru the silent sunlit sky

he briefly gazes
at me

as I watch

him
fly
by

spiraling thru space
untethered face to face
with madness and death

the mothership is gone
flown on, the earth behind me
upside down (would your sweet smile
be a frown) and in the distance
I see stars, the suns of other worlds

without direction I am free
without control I am controlled
by something I know nothing of

what is above, what is below
is this the everlasting flow
why don't I know what I should know
when will I come to where I go

I want to be with you
and see the sunrise in your eyes
and see the sunset there too

I want to see you bathed
in the light of a love that
is honest and true

I want to lay with you
under the open sky and
watch the clouds slowly
drift by ...

I want to lay with you
upon a bed of love and
sail away on waves of ecstasy

I want to see the beauty in you
and see the beauty in me, I want
to see the wisdom in you
and see the wisdom in me

I want to live with you
and die with you too
so we can fly away
together to some
great mystery

we live our lives

drifting down a river

between the shores of

comedy and tragedy

it is this daily journey
with its joys and sorrows,
highs and lows, that brings
us inevitably to a sea
of eternity ...

cherish the journey

wake up my friends

the night is gone and

today's adawn so

dance your dance

and sing your song

while the music of

life plays on
and on
and
on

a poet's wish

may this poem be a cup of water for the thirsty,

may this poem be a loaf of bread to feed the hungry,

may this poem be a warm embrace for those who feel
unloved or forlorn,

may this poem bring rest to the weary and comfort
to those who feel afflicted or resigned,

may this poem be a mirror to show us the ugliness of
greed and hatred,

may this poem be a mirror to show us the beauty of
love and sharing,

may this poem be a beacon that lights the way to
peace and wisdom for all mankind,

may this poem free our hearts and minds to
see we are all part of the divine,
which is always and everywhere, here
and there, now and forever
and we can cherish
each moment of
our lives together

the river's song

I've been sailing down this river
for so long, I've been sailing down
this river for so long,
then the rain came and
I wrote this song, yes
the rain came and I
wrote this song

now the water in this river
is getting strong, the water
in the river getting mighty
strong, and it won't be long,
no it won't be long, I'll be
part of the river's song,
the river's song ...

"I believe in nothing, everything is sacred.
I believe in everything, nothing is sacred."
TOM ROBBINS

"To the ordinary musician the sound is important.
To the master musician the silence is important:
he uses sound only to create silence."
OSHO

contact me on Facebook
"BLESSINGS OF ETERNITY"

Made in the USA
Middletown, DE
02 October 2015